T
W
OF THE
CROSS

FRANCES BIGGS
DONAL NEARY SJ

VERITAS

First published 2002 by
Veritas Publications
7/8 Lower Abbey Street
Dublin 1
Ireland
Email publications@veritas.ie
Website www.veritas.ie

Reprinted 2005

ISBN 1 85390 524 0

Design by Bill Bolger
Printed in the Republic of Ireland by Betaprint Ltd, Dublin

*Veritas books are printed on paper made from the wood pulp of managed forests. For
every tree felled, at least one tree is planted, thereby renewing natural resources.*

Introduction

In The Way of the Cross we can enter into the last journey of Jesus. Many artists have given their interpretation of the events which these stations recall. Frances Biggs has done this through her lived experience of the passion of Jesus. The text draws on one person's reflection on Frances' art, the stations themselves, and the ways in which Jesus still lives his passion and death today.

This booklet may be used for personal prayer, especially in Holy Week. It may be used as a reflection for a public stations of the cross in a church on Good Friday.

If used in public, the usual prayer to begin the stations may be used:

We adore you O Christ and we bless you,
because by your holy cross you have redeemed the world.
Glory be to the Father and to the Son and to the Holy Spirit, as it was in the
beginning, is now and ever shall be, world without end. Amen.

We pray the stations in horror sometimes at the terrible suffering of Jesus; in amazement that this suffering was caused by other men and women; in solidarity with the men and women who suffered with him; and always in thanks for what he has done for us.

We pray the stations in horror sometimes at the terrible suffering of Jesus in his people today; in amazement that this suffering is being caused by others, and in solidarity with the millions who suffer hardship in life today; and in thanks for those who still give their lives for bettering and saving the lives of their fellowmen and women.

Donal Neary SJ

1 Jesus is Condemned to Death

The boy is taking part in injustice and hatred
and doesn't even know it.
So often that can happen.
Our taxes may go to purchase arms which will kill the poor;
our words add to gossip destructive of the good name of another.
Unknown to ourselves
we may pour the water of condemnation.

Pilate is caught between guarding his job and prestige,
and doing what is right and just.
Don't we all know it's difficult to do the right thing
when others are pressurising us to do
what is less good, what is wrong?

I wonder did both of them see in Jesus' eyes
his conviction and love?
Love was stronger than the fear of what was to come.

Had Jesus not wondered and feared
that it would come to something like this;
and as he left Pilate,
did he know it would get worse?
And did he have the faith
that the condemnation to death
would lead him to the gift of new life?

We adore you, Christ our Lord and Saviour,
we praise your name in suffering and death;
Lord in your mercy, hear our prayer.

JESUS IS CONDEMNED
TO DEATH

2   Jesus Takes Up His Cross

A lone moment while we focus just on Jesus.
He is not given the cross, nor loaded with it.
Placed on the back that never asked for it,
the body already broken and bruised,
Jesus was actively accepting his cross.

Don't we know people who have done this?
Who have accepted fully the cross of life,
or who have allowed themselves suffer for others.

It's a lonely moment to accept a cross:
when you know that you are terminally ill,
when you know a loved one has truly left you,
when you know the loss of bereavement, failure, rejection,
when you allow yourself enter loneliness and pain,
when you suffer through any mistake you made in life.

And the difference is
that none of us need take our cross alone.
God carries our cross with us,
as he carried it with his Son.
Others help us too,
the people who care for us in our lives,
who help us take up our crosses.
They are the care and love of Jesus for us.

Lord teach me to know you more, love you more
and serve you more faithfully in my life.
Lord in your mercy, hear our prayer.

JESUS TAKES UP
HIS CROSS

3   Jesus Falls the First Time

Did any of them help the man on the ground?
Or did they just watch?
Observing, judging, afraid of another's fall;
only one face looks at him.

That's the way often;
people fall in different ways and we watch,
love gone wrong, exploitation in work,
or people forced out of home or country.
Or sin we hoped we could get over,
faults and failings which are always part of life.

He seems to be getting up from his fall,
his hand supporting him, and the face a bit crushed.
Maybe he knows that there's no help around him
and he must go it alone for another while.

Have you ever needed a hand,
like he needed a hand,
and all they did was watched?
Or talked about your pain from a distance?
He knows what it was like for you,
and then you know there is a hand always there,
the hand of God wounded but comforting.

Lead us not into temptation,
and when we find ourselves fallen,
raise us up on the path of life.
Lord in your mercy, hear our prayer.

JESUS FALLS
BENEATH THE CROSS

Jesus Meets His Mother

He didn't really 'meet' her – she was there;
and not by chance.
She wanted to be with her Son
even though it would be the cruellest moment of her life.
She didn't have to be there;
just like a parent doesn't have to be in the hospital all night with a child;
just like the child doesn't have to be with the parent who is ill;
just like the sister doesn't have to visit the brother in prison.
We visit in times of trouble from love:
visits of love, stations of love.

He didn't have to stop either;
it would be enough just to go on,
just to think of himself and get this over and done with.
Knowing his mother was suffering so much –
this was one of the cruellest moments so far.
He didn't have to stop,
just like the man on the way home to the comfort of family
doesn't have to stop and help on the soup-run,
or the student on the way to a first-class degree
didn't have to stop and help the weaker one.

They both suffered so much,
she for him, and he for us.
So far, and there was more to come.

Be with us Lord when we are in trouble,
be with us as you were with Mary in her trouble.
Lord in your mercy, hear our prayer.

JESUS
MEETS HIS MOTHER

5   **Simon Helps Jesus to Carry the Cross**

He seems to be telling Jesus to let go the cross
and he would carry it for him.
Simon – a person who wants to help,
to ease the burden, carry the load,
his sons knew Jesus, so he had probably met him.

Many are like that,
people giving a helping hand in financial trouble,
donating an organ of the body for another's health,
men and women carrying the cross for each other.

Simon seems to be willing to do this.
The others watch,
and maybe one of them takes a step forward to help.
Suffering brings out compassion in us.

And Jesus?
Glad to be helped, comforted,
to know that his suffering was understood,
even without many words
but with a healing touch and a prayer,
and that in the crowd there was companionship,
as we know another's help in our
bereavement, illness, rejection, let-down.
Glad to know that somebody wanted to help.

Open our arms Lord to help with the crosses of others,
and then we know we are helping carry your cross.
Lord in your mercy hear our prayer.

SIMON HELPS JESUS
TO CARRY THE CROSS

Veronica Wipes the Face of Jesus

He needed help.
The way of the cross is a journey of stops and stations,
each a station on the way of suffering.

We need doctors and nurses when we are ill,
counsellors and listeners at times of confusion,
social workers to get us through other times;
parents and family and friends to console us in bad times;
we are dependent on others from the start of life to its end
and Jesus was no different.

Someone came from the crowd with a towel,
something that would make life that little bit better
even for a while.
The towel offered coolness,
maybe a special towel from Veronica's house,
and the hand that gave it offered care.

Can we stop on the way of life
and be Veronica, a name known forever,
because she gave help to a suffering man?

When we help at a time of suffering
we are never forgotten.

Lord, help us to remember how we have helped others,
and been helped in our own lives.
Deepen in us the desire to help others.
Lord, in your mercy, hear our prayer.

VERONICA WIPES
THE FACE OF JESUS

7 Jesus Falls Again

It's worse the second time;
to fall, to fail, to feel ousted in some way,
and you feel you'll never succeed again,
you'll never find peace or strength again.
An illness come back, love fails once again,
and you know what it's like to fall the second time.

People pay less attention then;
Jesus falls and there's nobody around.
Simon has been sent back,
Veronica is in the crowd,
a second fall is a lonely fall.

There must have been sympathy in the crowd;
maybe somehow he noticed someone crying,
or someone praying for him.
You never know the good you can do
with a simple act of kindness,
a simple smile or encouraging presence,
a prayer for someone in trouble.

Even though he seemed to rise alone,
he rose with the strength of people in the crowd
who loved him, prayed for him, encouraged him.

Lord, when we fall, raise us up.
When we fall, send companions to raise us up.
May we raise up all who are bowed down.
Lord in your mercy hear our prayer.

JESUS FALLS
THE SECOND TIME

Some women prayed and looked for him –
a risky step out of the crowd.
Who knows whether they will be victimised later
for these simple few moments of sympathy
or maybe their families will be harassed –
'He's the son of the mad woman who followed Jesus'?

From the centre of his pain and suffering
Jesus recognised their pain.
Somehow their world had been shattered
with his condemnation and his death.
When a good man is killed our hope can die,
and when a good man is punished, we are all punished.

He spoke to their pain;
their pain of not being able to do very much,
even their fear of their own anguish and tears.

Physical pain recognising interior pain,
and knowing this could get worse,
like sensing that war will get worse
or violence will increase and influence
the lives of our grandchildren.
This short station gave courage to both;
the women could live stronger having met him,
and he walked on stronger knowing others cared.

Lord, send comforters and consolers to all who are ill,
to all who are in pain and to all who suffer.
Lord, in your mercy, hear our prayer.

JESUS SPEAKS TO THE
WOMEN OF JERUSALEM

9 Jesus Falls the Third Time

On this fall he seems to fall farther into the ground.

It makes us wonder how we can stand by and watch,
as someone else is victimised.
It happens on streets often when people are mugged,
or in families when others know there is abuse,
or in a school where bullying by teachers or pupils is ignored;
or gossip spreads lies and we can't find the way to stop it.

When good people can do little or nothing,
evil flourishes and people fall by the wayside.

Or people fall and need help to get up,
and it's more difficult the third time:
the boy or girl on the third attempt to get off drugs,
the woman or man trying to get free of alcohol,
the students who fail to study year after year.

Life can make us fragile
and the fall on the way
may be the push we got when we were
bullied or abused or slandered years ago.
We fall and rise on our own way of the cross,
and on his way up he raises us up.

Lord, you have been raised by the power of the Spirit,
you are the Saviour of the world.
Raise us up in courage when we fall.
Lord, in your mercy, hear our prayer.

JESUS FALLS
THE THIRD TIME

10 Jesus is Stripped of His Garments

There seems to be horror on the faces of those who watch,
as the indignity of a stripping is carried out.
There's the physical pain of clothes being torn
and the other pain of being naked in public.

We think of many who share the same fate:
men and women strip-searched,
people who have been abused and raped,
people whose bodies have been exploited
in violence, pornography, medical science.

The soldiers needed to steel their feelings,
as we can dull our response to the pain of others.

Others watched:
maybe the friend who made the clothes in love,
the mother who bathed the body as a baby,
the friends who hugged the face of Jesus.
Did he remember these as he suffered at this station?

Memories of tenderness and comfort from others
get us through moments of indignity and pain;
memories of faith with God enliven us
in moments when we wonder if God is absent.

Lord your dignity was stripped by the violence of others;
we pray for all who suffer abuse of any sort,
whose dignity is robbed by the greed of others,
Lord in your mercy, hear our prayer.

JESUS IS STRIPPED
OF HIS CLOTHES

11 Jesus is Nailed to the Cross

So different from how we like to think of death;
we wonder was Jesus unconscious as they nailed him.
Hardly – pain would have wakened him from any sedation,
as the nails were hammered through his flesh given for us.

We can say that Jesus is nailed to the cross today –
just think of how we would hear
the sound of the nails in human cries:

millions starving, undernourished, hungry;
men and women imprisoned for the cause of justice;
the people living at the side of the road
or sleeping rough in our cities,
the meaninglessness in life leading to addiction,
the lack of love leading to casual relationships
and many ways people are not happy or content.

When others suffer Jesus is still nailed to the cross.

It's good for us to wince at the pain of others' lives.
And we watch – again the observers watch;
as pain kept Jesus from unconsciousness,
may the pain of others keep us awake
to the urgent pain of God nailed to modern crosses.

As you searched for the love and will of your father
in your worst times of pain, dear Lord,
let us know the presence of your Father in our pain.
Lord, in your mercy, hear our prayer.

JESUS IS NAILED
TO THE CROSS

12 Jesus Dies on the Cross

The faces are sad, grieving, desolate;
isn't that what death can do to us?
And more so when death is
inflicted by humans on another human?

Was Mary praying a line from her Magnificat,
'He casts the mighty from their thrones and raises the lowly'?
Or was John remembering words like
'I will raise you up on the last day'?

And Jesus — he seems to find trust and faith in this hour:
faith that his Father would not abandon him,
faith that the thief — out of sight just now —
would find happiness that day;
faith that John and Mary would care for each other.
And the women — was their faith strengthened
by the love they felt from Mary and John?

Recall that this picture has for centuries
helped millions through the darkest hour;
we know now what Jesus knew at the end of it all:
that others were with him to the end.
and maybe he knew that others were at a distance,
and that God is close and promises life forever.

Holy Mary mother of God,
be with us in the worst of times,
pray for us, sinners,
now and at the hour of our death. Amen.

JESUS
DIES ON THE CROSS

It all seems more gentle now.
Carried by friends into the future;
the hands and heart of God
touching and consoling him,
in the hands and hearts of
a parent, a friend, a follower.

Is there ever a time when we are unconnected?
Even in death, we need others,
and while death is the most lonely moment –
or seems so –
it's often the time we're most surrounded by love.
Did he not know that he was cared for now?
And maybe he knew all along the away
that these people cared but couldn't reach him.

As they took him down gently,
they tell us to take others down gently,
at bad times of life and love and illness.
People live on many crosses –
illness, loss, rejection, oppression
and we need those who want to take them down,
consolers and helpers at all sorts of bad times,
and lay them where life will be fuller and kinder.

When pain and suffering is over, Lord and Saviour,
make us truly grateful
for all who have stood by us in bad times.
Lord, in your mercy, hear our prayer.

JESUS IS TAKEN DOWN
FROM THE CROSS

14 The Body of Jesus is Laid in the Tomb

There's care and love among them all
as they look on the one who has been sacrificed.
A mother's love lasting through the falls and the violence,
and the followers who can't understand it all,
but are willing to give their hands and hearts to help.

Love doesn't always try to understand,
love can get into action before knowing why
and only in the doing is the knowing.
Often only love can reason why.

In getting involved, they got to know God.
For it was God they were holding:
the creator of the universe had become the servant,
and the servant had loved to the end.

Never again will the word 'tomb' mean the same,
for now because of Jesus the tomb
is the home of resurrection and life,
as every grave and urn promise new life.

The body is dead; the spirit is alive.
Love has conquered all
and in love faith and hope can still exist.

Give us patience Lord to know that
joy and life follow suffering and death;
and the peace of knowing
that your love will never fail us.

THE BODY OF JESUS
IS LAID IN THE TOMB